AF265367

I Remember

I Remember

by Luda Shuster

Luda Shuster
I Remember

Copyright © 2019 by Luda Shuster
All Rights Reserved

Art Director: Laura J. Testa-Reyes, Catalyst
Creations West
First Printing 2019

Printed in the United States of America
This book is published by Luda Shuster. No
part of this book may be reproduced in any
form or used in any manner whatsoever
without the express written permission of
the publisher except for the use of brief
quotations in a book review or scholarly
journal.

Please contact the author if you would like
permission to use any portion of this book.
Published in the United States of America
by Service for Profit, LLC

ISBN-13: 9780578470306

To my family, past, present and future

Ибо время, столкнувшись с памятью, узнает о своем бесправии.

—Joseph Brodsky

Having bumped into memory, time learns its impotence.

Table of Contents

My Childhood Family

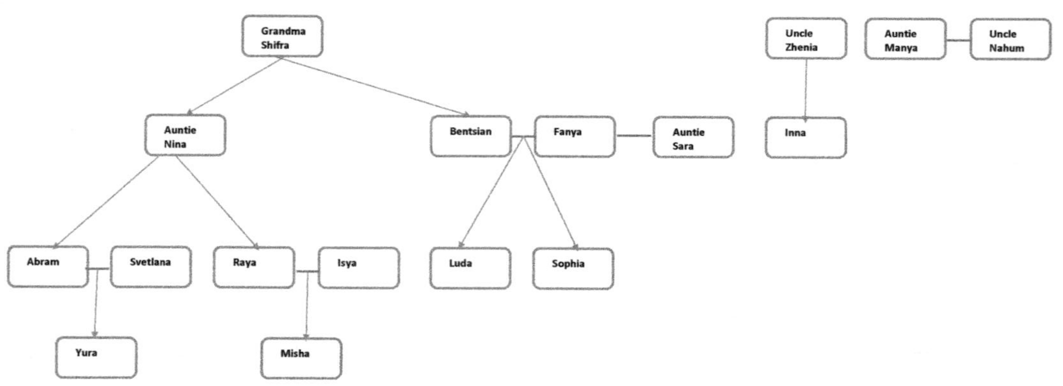

-1-

My Naive Parents

1952 was an interesting year in Russia. The great friend of the people, Joseph Stalin, conceived the Soviet version of a final solution to the Jewish problem.

Jewish names were figuring prominently in the newspapers

next to such terms as rootless cosmopolites and poisoning doctors. These articles were collectively discussed at meetings and were unanimously approved by the workers. Doctors, lawyers and managers with Jewish names were losing their jobs. There were rumors about expelling all Jews to the newly created Jewish autonomous republic in the Far East, to be saved from the rightful anger of the Soviet people. Jews with a good grasp of reality were gathering warm clothes and suitcases. It was just a matter of time.

In the meantime, my parents, a Jewish couple living in the

city of Gomel, were blissfully unaware of the big picture. Being from a very modest background,

My parents in 1947

neither had a friend or relative who had fallen victim to Stalin's purges. My father fought in the Patriotic War from 1941 to 1945, marching from Gomel to

Berlin. My mom lived through Leningrad's siege and starvation. Their world existed in a well-defined black and white palette. Hitler and fascists were the enemies. The Soviet Union was the only country where working people were not oppressed. Internal spies wanting to harm a young socialist country had to be flushed out and punished. My parents believed what they read in newspapers and heard on the radio. They discounted whispers of their Jewish neighbors. They had good jobs, my father a general counsel for one of the largest glass manufacturers in the country, my mother assistant district attorney for the city of Gomel.

Thus it came as a complete shock when one day in the summer of 1952, my mother was called by her boss and ordered to resign. Not understanding what was happening, she flatly refused. Well, said her boss, in this case we'll start gathering compromising material ("compromat" in the vernacular of those years). Such was my mom's firm belief in her innocence and in the rule of law, that she said: you do that. As it turned out, no compromat was needed. Instead, my mother was ordered to work at another city,

Vitebsk, leaving her husband and two small children behind. When she refused to follow that order, she was fired. I'm sure her boss wasn't a bad kind, he was just following orders. In 1952, losing one's job wasn't the worst thing. But again, my parents weren't seeing the bigger picture.

They decided to fight for justice the only way they knew how: appealing to the official rule of law. A long, carefully written letter was sent to Moscow, to the Chief Prosecutor Vyshinsky, Stalin's right hand in administering justice. A month later my mother was called to Moscow for an audience

with Vyshinsky's assistant.
Many accounts exist describing
such fateful audiences with
officials, where grievances were
voiced. More often than not,
the complaints ended in arrest,
jail sentence, camp term or
sometimes "10 years without
correspondence," that time's
euphemism for a death sentence.
The assistant benevolently
listened to my mom, asked her to
gather additional documentation,
and promised to call her back for
the final resolution of her case
after reviewing it. Documentation
was prepared and mailed, but no
invitation followed. Miraculously,
no sanctions followed either. My
parents got incredibly lucky – in

the dangerous political climate of that era, the mice got away with complaining about the cat's misbehavior.

The second final solution didn't happen after all. The immortal ruler kicked the bucket on March 5 1953. Mass Jewish exile to the Far East didn't come to pass. My parents were lucky, having successfully survived their foolish attempt at personal justice. Slowly they learned about "the other" history of Stalin's years, the one they hadn't known about. They continued to practice law and bring a measure of justice for other people in the world they lived in. Through our childhood, there was a constant stream of visitors in our house, friends and acquaintances who were coming for free legal advice.

The most memorable case was an unusual couple, she a cute diminutive Jewish woman, he a tall handsome man of Hungarian descent with a full head of dark hair and fiery eyes. For more than a year, they were frequent visitors and my sister and I learned their story as our parents were discussing their case and writing multiple appeals. They had met in prison. In the beginning of the war, she shared a bad dream with her friends, interpreting it as a forewarning of losing another city to German troops. That was enough to condemn her for anti-Soviet propaganda, followed by a multi-year jail sentence. His case was similarly fabricated. In the mid-50s, it became possible to appeal cases created during Stalin's regime. That is what my parents did for "Auntie and Uncle Gabor" as we called them. Many evening hours went into writing appeals, all of them free of charge. The hard work of my parents paid off when the Gabors' convictions were overturned and "crimes" expunged from their records – a very big deal at the time.

A quiet city cemetery in Gomel
has been the resting place for
our father's tortured soul for
almost 30 years now. Our mom
still nods to me and my sister
when we come to see her at a
San Francisco nursing home.
We like to think she recognizes
us. We also like to think that our
parents' stubborn faith in fairness
and justice lives on in us and our
children – and if we're lucky – in
our grandchildren as well.

14

-2-

Auntie Sara

The tea is finished, the floor is swept clean and the wind is beating at the window curtains as our train is speeding through Moscow suburb train stations. Our hearts are pounding as we recognize the familiar landscape. The train radio is playing "My dear capital, my golden Moscow!" Here comes the familiar announcement: "Comrades passengers, our train is arriving at the capital of our motherland, Moscow," and the train is slowly pulling into the noisy station.

Hurray! My sister and I are on our yearly summer vacation with our Auntie Sara who lives in Podolsk, a big industrial town near Moscow. Here she is, dressed up and accessorized, as usual, kissing us, picking up our suitcases. Sometimes she comes with her friend who has a car and we drive to Podolsk. Sometimes we catch the Moscow metro to get from one train station to another where we will catch a train to Podolsk. Then there is a

short walk from the station to
the old house and we are in our
summer paradise.

Ah, that special inimitable
smell of the old two-story
wooden house with its dark
airy corridors! Six families
upstairs, six families downstairs,
a kitchen on every floor with
men and women's bathrooms
downstairs. Colorful characters
inhabit this world, mostly blue
collar Russian folk, different from
predominantly Jewish neighbors
and friends we have at home
in Gomel. Children enjoy the
absolute freedom of roaming
through the house and two

adjacent spacious gardens where lilacs bloom all summer long.

In this house, our Auntie Sara has her own private room and a semiprivate kitchen which she shares with another family. Her room is a collection of many wonderful familiar things: a music box with its cheerful marching music, a full length mirror with the assortment of lipsticks and jewelry, and the most special for me, a bookcase that promises hours and hours of pages by Chekhov, Gogol, Tolstoy, Defoe and Cooper.

Both my sister and I have friends here and every summer we

reconnect and spend long warm blissful days together, running, playing games, gossiping or

Auntie Sara, Luda and Sophia in 1960

listening to grown-ups gossip. Adults often sit outside, either discussing other people's dirty laundry or playing a favorite Russian card game, "durak" (fool). Everything here is public – cooking, doing laundry in the common kitchen, going to the bathroom. Our auntie with her absurdly Jewish name is surrounded by ethnic Russians and is the subject of intense gossip, but never in our presence.

She holds an important position as head of the Podolsk Trade Commission's planning department. In a shortage besieged Soviet Union, her access to any kind of goods at the official low (not black market) prices makes her omnipotent. My sister Sophia and I feel like children of privilege anywhere we go. She can stretch a modest amount of rubles given by our mom to buy a bunch of nice clothes. Very often Auntie Sara kicks in her money to buy things we can't afford. The food we eat here is also special: caviar, salami, smoked fish and of course, the most improbable, ice cream cake.

Auntie Sara constantly helps other people through her vast chain of connections. She is suspected by her neighbors of taking millions in bribes. Years later, we understood our mom's repeated words about our family being "honest people." Auntie Sara was a rare exception in that black market economy, never taking bribes. Exception or not, we enjoyed all the perks we got through her – visiting Moscow, riding the metro, going to Bolshoi theatre and magnificent art museums. One of the millions of Soviet women left single by the war, Auntie Sara was a devoted daughter to our grandparents and devoted sister and auntie. She wanted us to have the best she could provide.

She liked discipline and order; my sister and I would get in trouble when we didn't do our easy chores on time. Being older and lazier, I was most often the recipient of her stern lectures.

Our mom was also slightly scared of critical remarks by her big sister. But mostly our time together was fun, and she was always lining up a list of interesting things to do. When we got older, we were allowed to go to Moscow on our own, and what outrageous fun it was to make a trip on an electric train, then on the metro, all on our own, using money to buy tickets like adults.

One of the visits we made every year was to the cemetery where our grandparents were buried. I remember even now the long bus ride to the cemetery, walking down familiar alleys, seeing familiar monuments

and greenery on the old graves
growing wilder every year.
It would be a no-nonsense
housekeeping visit, where we
would wash the photographs on
stones and bring flowers. Russian
cemeteries have fences around
the graves, and painting the fence

Our maternal grandparents Efim and
Anyuta circa 1925

was one of the upkeep items as well. If our mom was there, she could tear up, but never Auntie Sara.

We know little about our maternal grandparents. Our grandmother died when I was four and grandfather followed her a year later. Born at the end of the nineteenth century, they lived through the First World War, Russian revolution, Russian Civil War, first bombs of the Second World War, evacuation from the city of Gomel to Siberia with the last train and then returning to Podolsk. Not even having school diplomas, always on the cusp of poverty, they were determined to give their daughters higher education. Scrimping on everything, they sent Auntie Sara to Leningrad School of Economy and our mom to Leningrad Law School. We heard that our grandma Anyuta (Hannah) was a leader in the family, strict with children and a devoted friend. Our grandpa Efim (Chaim) was a kind loving man, devoted to his wife and family.

Sometimes I imagine how dreadful my sister's and my childhood would have been, had it not been for Auntie Sara. In those happy summer months, we forgot about our uneasy family life, eternal money problems, school and homework. Help from her was also constant and substantial throughout the rest of the year: our first refrigerator and TV came from her; when years were especially difficult,

Sisters Sara (left) and Fanya circa 1940

she would be sending us food parcels. For me, she was buying books and I still remember that magical moment of opening the parcel and seeing the words "Doctor Doolittle" on a bright cover.

When I entered the University of Moscow, Auntie Sara became my home base, where I could get a respite from dorm life. Especially important at that age, thanks to her, my clothes were always cool and trendy, bought at unheard of "real" prices, not black market ones. Auntie Sara was truly my anchor of stability during those years, while family life at Gomel was becoming increasingly unpredictable and dangerous for my mom and sister.

When I graduated, Auntie Sara obtained "propiska" – the right to live and work in Moscow, a precious thing in Russia of that time, first for me and then for my husband. It literally changed our lives, enabling us to hold Moscow jobs, the right we didn't have as we weren't born "Muscovites."

It was then that Auntie Sara discovered a tumor in her breast but kept it a secret from everybody, not wanting to burden other people with her troubles. She was only in her early fifties but she sought medical help too late. Brutal surgery was the only thing that could be done at that point. It extended her life by three years. Auntie Sara died in the fall of

Cousins Zhenia (right) and Sasha at Podolsk cemetery in 1987

1975 at the age of 55. We laid her to rest at the same grave where our grandparents were buried. At her funeral, both my sister and I were pregnant with our daughters, Zhenia and Sasha, who were born five months later, 28 hours apart.

Thirty-three years later, in another century and country, my daughter gave birth to a little girl and called her Athena Sara. She had heard the stories about Auntie Sara and decided to keep the name in the family. Every time I hear "Athena Sara," a little breeze of recognition runs down my spine and I'm grateful again and again that we have an everyday reminder of our auntie in our granddaughter.

The only time I remember seeing Auntie Sara crying was when she saw us off at the railroad station leaving for Gomel. The arrival ritual would be reversed, and we would be sitting in front of the train's window, suitcases full of presents, eating the "last" ice cream she would buy for us at the station. Gone was the stern disciplinarian, it was our loving auntie with whom we were parting. After all practical advice had been dispensed (don't get off at the train stops, be careful with the hot tea, don't forget to write), we would grow silent and just stare at each other as if wanting to memorize the faces. And in the last minute, all of us would break down crying, trying to hide it. I can see her right now in my mind's eye, as the train slowly starts moving and she walks a little bit keeping up with our moving car, but the train speeds up and she stands there waving, and we try to look at her for as long as we can, until the station is left far behind. Farewell, Auntie Sara, your memory is with us always.

-3-

Auntie Nina

Yay, Auntie Nina is here – a familiar kindly face with a few wrinkles on still smooth cheeks, huge glasses and bottomless black bag. She never comes empty-handed, most often bringing home-baked goodies or a bit of sweet syrup.

My sister and I love her visits,
as they always promise fun and
entertainment. Auntie Nina
tells us about our grandmother
Shifra's latest antics and demands
as well as news about our cousins
Abram and Raya. For us kids, it
feels like theatre, listening and
watching as she uses her hands
and whole body, familiar voice
with a sing-song intonation
going up and down as the story
unfolds. Sometimes Auntie
Nina recalls the past, telling us
how in 1941 she was evacuated
from Gomel to Sverdlovsk with
two small children, mother and
brother, while her husband
Zyama, Raya's and Abram's
father, was drafted and perished

at the very beginning of the war. Auntie Nina tells her stories with such pathos that we cry and laugh with her. Almost always she complains about Shifra, who is both her aunt and stepmother and lives with her.

Shifra is remembered as an evil spirit by everybody in our family – her children, grandchildren and our mom. Her demanding

Our paternal grandmother Shifra circa 1950

nature, mean spirit and selfishness are legendary. Our mom remembered forever the episode of being very sick with a high fever and staying home from work. Shifra berated her: "You have no business lounging around like a lady, get up!" Shifra forbade Auntie Nina to share food with her children and criticized her mercilessly.

I know about Shifra's horrible character from other people's stories. She raised me for the first four years of my life and I felt nothing but love from her. Maybe because my sister and I were the youngest granddaughters by her youngest son, Bentsian, or for

some other reason, we never saw
the mean side of her personality.
Whenever we visited her, she was
so happy to see us, hugging and
touching us as if to confirm our
well-being. Later, with children's
cruelty, we would mimic her
sighs and distress on finding
out that our underwear was not
warm enough to her standards.

Auntie Nina would visit our
house once a month or so, and
once in a while, my sister and
I would go and visit her and
grandma Shifra at their small
barrack-style apartment, made
a little bit more comfortable by
ingenuity and the smart hands of
our cousin Abram.

Children are not only cruel, they don't pay too much attention to the people around them. Most of the stuff I know about Auntie Nina I learned and understood later. Having lost her mother at a very early age, she had to help her aunt and stepmother, Shifra, raise her younger brothers. Her childhood came at the beginning of the 20th century, one of the most tumultuous periods in Russian history: first world war, Bolshevik revolution, civil war, poverty and deprivation. Her father, my paternal grandfather Simon, disappeared sometime in 1913, after my father was born, leaving Shifra behind with five young children. The family legend says Simon was a smart man, a math teacher, not an observant Jew and almost certainly mentally ill.

Having raised her brothers, Auntie Nina married Zyama Yuditsky and had two kids,

Auntie Nina with her husband Zyama circa 1930

Abram and Raya. They were a happy couple, leading a modest life in Gomel where Zyama was a barber. When the war of 1941 started, he was immediately drafted and perished in the first year of the war. Nina and her family were evacuated to Sverdlovsk, and the cycle of war and deprivation repeated itself.

Having read a lot about what befell them, I try to imagine what Auntie Nina and Grandma Shifra had to do to survive. Perhaps Shifra would have been a nicer person had she had an easier life. Becoming mean could have just been her response to incredible hardships.

Life full of deprivation and back-
breaking work didn't toughen
up Auntie Nina. There was not a
mean bone in her body. I've never
seen her angry. Crying, yes, when
Shifra wouldn't let her share food
with Abram and Raya or when
she remembered her husband,
never about herself. Her devotion
to family had no boundaries. I
remember her sharing a secret
with us once: Raya suspected
that Abram (a bachelor at that
time) was somewhat squeamish
about her newborn son Misha
(why wouldn't he be scared of
handling a squirming newborn?).
That kind of discord between
her children would upset her,
never ongoing hardships of her

own life. She was devoted to my father, even when he didn't want to see her. She was the only one maintaining a relationship with all of her brothers who weren't that interested in each other.

I remember once bumping into her in the bathhouse line, reading a Jewish newspaper. I never suspected she not only spoke Yiddish but could read it also. I never asked how she got her hands on that newspaper – a lack of curiosity that I regret so much now.

In the sixties, after many years of living in a barrack-style dwelling with no conveniences,

Auntie Nina and Grandma
Shifra (oh, Soviet miracle) got
a one-bedroom apartment with
plumbing and hot water, the first
ever in their lives.

Soon afterwards, Shifra came
down with dementia and Auntie
Nina, who was in her sixties then
and not in great health herself,
placed her in a nursing home.
Visiting there after a few weeks,
she overheard Shifra, then almost
deaf and confused, cry and beg
for help. That day, Auntie Nina
took Shifra back home and
nursed her until the very end.

Her fate seemed to be that of
a continuous caregiver, first

brothers, then children, then stepmother. Sadly, she didn't have much time left for herself. Auntie Nina died in 1970 from pancreatic cancer. She remained stoic up till the very end, never complaining.

Looking at her pictures now, I realize she was quite a looker, with high cheekbones, which were still there at middle age when I knew her.

Auntie Nina's resting place is in Gomel's cemetery. Centrifugal forces of history brought Raya's family to Israel, and Abram's family (after his death in 1989) landed in California. Raya's grandson, Sagi, moved even further away from his ancestral continent, landing in Australia. And it's there, in Australia, in May of 2018, that Auntie Nina's great-great-grandson, little Elton, was born. When I get to meet him, he will be the sixth generation of this family I get to know. Auntie Nina's family story is a microcosm of my tribe's peripatetic history, where change is constant, be it country or language or vocations, but also constant is a fierce desire to belong and share in the destiny of Jewish people.

Kind, loving Auntie Nina, I often remember her, how courageously

and steadfastly she carried her
life load and how much warmth
and kindness she added to the
lives of all of us.

-4-

Auntie Manya

Auntie Manya was part of our Gomel life. Technically, she was our grand aunt, but we always called her Auntie Manya. She and her husband Nahum lived in a small house on the street of Paris Commune about three miles from us. We saw her a few times a year; sometimes she would visit, sometimes my sister and I would go over to their house. That place with low ceilings and small windows always reminded me of Gogol's "The Old World Landowners" (Старосветские помещики) story about a firmly established sleepy flow of life, with all interests revolving around basic needs. They augmented their meager pensions by tending a small garden and vegetable patch and renting one of their rooms.

Once a year she invited us to Passover dinner with matzah, sweet wine and gefilte fish, but nothing was said about Passover, it was just a festive meal with an unusual menu and booze. My memory kept the glimmer of small silver wine glasses, gefilte fish smell, Nahum's jokes about wanting bread and Auntie Manya shushing him. I guess that was our only exposure to Jewish tradition.

Here's a bit of my maternal grandfather's family history as we know it. Three Plotkin siblings were born at the end of the nineteenth century: elder brother, Evel (rendered in Russian as Zhenia), sister Maria (Manya) and younger brother Chaim (Efim), my maternal grandfather. They were probably born in Gomel. Uncle Zhenia was a clever one, with a good command of the Russian language (in addition to family Yiddish) and was good with writing and math. At one point, Zhenia moved to Moscow, found a good job in supply management and married a very pretty girl. They had a son, Simon, and daughter, Inna. Manya and Efim stayed behind in Gomel. Manya married Nahum Gurevich and they had a son Simon. Efim married my grandmother Hanna (Anyuta), they had two daughters: my aunt Sara and my mom Fanya.

Not sure how Nahum made a living, but they were well off, doing better than our grandparents. Manya worshipped her older brother Zhenia, but was not very attached to my grandfather, a kind gentle guy, somewhat naive and completely devoted to his family. He was a sales clerk in a store and their life was very modest.

When the Great Patriotic War of 1941 started, Simon Plotkin and Simon Gurevich were drafted immediately. We know that one of them was a tank driver. Both of them perished in the war. My memories of Auntie Manya and

Uncle Zhenia with his daughter Inna start in the middle of the 1950s, more than ten years after the war. By then, uncle Zhenia's wife has been long dead and so was my grandfather Efim, the youngest of the siblings.

Uncle Zhenia and Inna were part of our Moscow life. We would visit them once a year, while spending summer vacation with Auntie Sara in Podolsk. This visit was always special: traveling on the metro, then entering a huge multistory building in the center of Moscow right across from the metro station, which was built before the revolution for rich families. In the Soviet time, one apartment in such a building would house 5 to 8 families, each having their own room and sharing a toilet, bathroom and kitchen. On the big entrance door, there was a row of ringing bell buttons, each with the family's name next to it. I remember a long corridor in a humongous communal apartment, the doors on the right and on the left, kitchen with multiple tables.

In this apartment, Uncle Zhenia and his daughter Inna, who was a music teacher, lived in a spacious room with an alcove and a big bay window overlooking a large square. Family legend had it that Inna, who was quite a looker, used this square as a meeting place with her multiple admirers. She would use her binoculars to make sure the guy was there and waiting, prior to heading out. That was before our time though. My memory kicks in when she was around 30, a spinster by Russian standards. We heard she was too finicky, and with so many men killed in the war, she ended up single.

That huge room with a very tall ceiling and elaborate molding served as a bedroom, living room and dining room. I remember old fashioned solid furniture: a huge table, part of which served as a dining table; a bookshelf where

I first found and read Alexander Blok's poetry; an old piano with knick-knacks on it. Inna was a casual housekeeper, so the room was always somewhat messy, but, in my mind, there was Moscow grandeur to it. Both Inna and Uncle Zhenia treated us with benevolent condescension, the way one would treat remote provincial relatives (which we were). Being a cultured Muscovite, Inna sometimes took us to the Bolshoi theatre, a treat of the highest order. This is how we saw our first opera, "Sadko." In general, she was cordial, but not that interested in us.

Somewhere in the late 60s, when I was already at school in Moscow, Auntie Manya's house in Gomel was demolished and she got an apartment with all the amenities. Soon afterwards Nahum died and Auntie Manya was alone.

This was an exceptionally hard time in our family history. With an abusive father at home, my mom and sister, fearing for their lives, spent many nights outside of their house, crashing in small Soviet apartments of my mom's friends. At one point, my mom asked Auntie Manya to allow us to live with her. As with other important matters, Auntie asked her older brother, Uncle Zhenia, for advice. My mom saw the letter he wrote back to his sister. One of the sentences went like this: "Who is she (my mom) to you, that you have to help her?" Auntie Manya dutifully followed her brother's advice. From that point on, the ties with Auntie

Sisters Sophia (left) and Luda circa 1954

Manya and Uncle Zhenia were broken. I remember only one phone call my mom made in September 1975 to tell Inna that Auntie Sara had died. That was it.

Our maternal grand-father Efim Plotkin, 1888-1954

Out of the three Plotkin siblings, only the youngest one, simpleton Efim, was granted grandchildren, my sister and myself. He died first, at 65, of a broken heart, a year after his wife's, my maternal grandmother's death. Uncle Zhenia and Auntie Manya lived well into their eighties. Were they bitter toward fate refusing them progeny? Or maybe they never liked Efim to begin with. We will never know.

Looking back, I try to rationalize this story to extract some meaning.

Sayings like "family first" and "blood is thicker than water" sound good but sharing genetic material is not a guarantee of devotion or love or even just getting along. The nature of family relationships is tricky and often impossible to predict or explain, but family history isn't complete without it. Along with blood lines, it should include our likes, antipathies, examples of utter devotion and sheer indifference.

Sometimes it takes a strong vision to filter out the flotsam and jetsam of everyday life to recognize those family bonds that are true and matter. In the moments of absolute clarity, they make our hearts sing.

And what about other cases where genetics aren't enough? Sometimes they fill us with sadness, sometimes they make us angry, sometimes we just shrug and ignore nature's unfulfilled promise of kinship.

-5-

Nature Girl

I remember the day my daughter came home from Girl Scout camp with a tale of woe: On a Foothill Park outing she was stung by a bee. Soaking in my comforting kisses, she affected some melodramatic sobs and said with deep conviction, "Mom,

I'm not a nature girl." I had to restrain myself from a smile. How could my daughter have even thought she was a nature girl, really, seriously!

I always hated nature. "Nature" was our garden and vegetable patch – to be weeded many times during summer. Nature was school organized outings to nearby woods, where other kids seemed to have fun and where I was counting minutes. There were beetles I was afraid of, nice looking but definitely poisonous mushrooms, prickly fir trees and absolutely not one clean place to sit down.

I suppose it didn't help that
our parents were city people,
professionally and by taste. The
garden was just to provide our
family with the vitamins for long
Russian winters. State stores
could be counted on to carry
only cabbage and potatoes. The
open market next to our house
carried all kinds of wonderful
goodies but we didn't have that
kind of money. In other words,
nature was all work and boring.
I used to think that admiration of
nature was one giant hypocrisy
perpetrated by writers and
crazy people who liked to climb
mountains, backpack in the
wilderness and in general subject
themselves to ridiculous weather

conditions. While consoling my daughter in her nature mishap, I was thanking my lucky stars for living in the U.S. and not needing to grow food, go camping or whatever else people do outside.

Later that fall I had to go on a business trip to the East Coast. In the excitement of preparation, I was ignoring our secretary's grumbling about "foliage" and not being able to find a hotel in Massachusetts. It was late at night when the plane landed in Boston, and there was a long taxi ride to my hotel in New Hampshire where I ended up staying. Next morning, my colleague picked me up and we caught I-128 to be at work early.

The October sun was slowly rising in the sky as red, green, yellow, golden, brown and purple trees were appearing from the darkness. It was a symphony, a blizzard, an attack of color. I couldn't take my eyes off those trees. They were beautiful. They were overwhelming. They spoke to me. Why at that moment? Why not in my first 30 autumns in Russia? Did I need six years of carefully measured California fall palette to sharpen my vision? Was there a silent part of me finally claiming its own place in my psyche? Did it even matter?

The cataract was gone, and ever since nature has been a constant presence in my life.

I also instantly knew the answer to the question: Are you a mountain person or ocean person or forest person? Mountains and oceans are awesome but it's the trees that talk to me.

Next year on a warm April day, a radioactive cloud of unknown origin was noticed over Scandinavia and "Chernobyl" became a household name. In horror, I read about winds blowing radioactive clouds toward the city of Gomel where my mom and my sister's family still lived. My little niece and nephew under radioactive rain! I made frantic calls to the Stanford physics department. Could I buy a Geiger counter? Would it help my family? How can they protect themselves? The answers were benevolently vague and noncommittal. The news was full of conflicting opinions and predictions. I needed to warn my family, while being careful about what I said – according to the media, people there were not told immediately about the catastrophe and international calls were being monitored. Disclosing information could have consequences. Powers that be could stop me from ever seeing my family again. "How is life, what's new" were the questions I was asking my mom and sister, and they were careful and nervously neutral in their responses. "Just don't drink milk!" I screamed in desperation as we were saying our goodbyes on the phone – knowing that radioactive particles were slowly making their way up the food chain.

Three years later, my family emigrated to the U.S. I never set foot in the icky forests of my childhood again. Nor will I ever be able to. In the aftermath of Chernobyl, those woods are radioactive now, full of mutant plants and animals. There is a picture in an old photo album showing me during one of my school outings, standing in front of a prickly fir tree. I don't look happy, a nature hating teenager surrounded by the woods, then unloved and now verboten.

Luda in 1961

-6-

Saturday Visit

As usual, I pick mom up around 1 pm and at once we start bickering about who will be choosing the restaurant. I want her to choose and she wants me to do it. Finally I say "what about that place you had salmon cakes last time," and she immediately

agrees. Sometimes I think that she
really knows where she wants
to go and just waits for me to
make the right guess. Four weeks
ago we had lunch in Menlo
Park at "Late for the Train" and
she fainted afterwards, creating
quite a commotion among the
staff. My husband was sure they
would refuse service to us after
that incident, but waiters had
other things on their minds.
The restaurant had just changed
owners and was closing in two
weeks. Anyway, it was probably
a very large meal for her (two
humongous blintzes) that caused
the faint. Salmon cakes on
Saturday went down just fine.

This time babushka (her usual
family name) chooses blintzes
again but eats only one, her usual
portion. I ask if she wants to walk
afterwards and she says she *really*
wants to show me their fitness
center. Since this is the second
time she mentions it, I say yes.
Then I remember that I was going
to buy her a book of English
poetry, to exercise memory,
and ask her if it's OK to go to a
bookstore. She says yes but she
will stay in the car – it's too hard
to get in and out. Our schedule
for today is set: lunch, bookstore,
fitness center, then her apartment.
I drive to California Avenue to
"Know Knew Books" and find
great street parking in the shade.

With Eugene Onegin playing on
the CD player so babushka will
not be bored while waiting, I run
into the store.

The children's book department
is in the back, and the floor
is strewn with books big and
small. I pick a nice Mother Goose
edition with beautiful Hague's
illustrations and return to the
car. Babushka immediately dives
into the book making hilarious
guesses about what some words
and verses mean. She looks
pleased with it. I tell her the
quota will be one verse a day, she
has to memorize it and recite it
to me. She finds "rain, rain, go
away, come again another day,"

and is completely taken with the task of memorization. She repeats it again and again closing her eyes. By the time we turn onto University Avenue, she nails it.

Now she takes me to the fitness center through their cheery yard with blooming trees and sweet smells of spring. The room is full of machines adapted to a senior crowd. Babushka sits down at the low wide-seat bike, a pretty safe contraption. Another person in the room is an elderly Asian woman on a stationary bike. Babushka says in Russian, "I know her husband" and then repeats the same in English to the woman. She answers back something nice but I don't understand because of the strong accent. I sit on the chair and look at them, pushing bike pedals side by side in the fitness center of the American senior home, such a mundane scene in contrast with

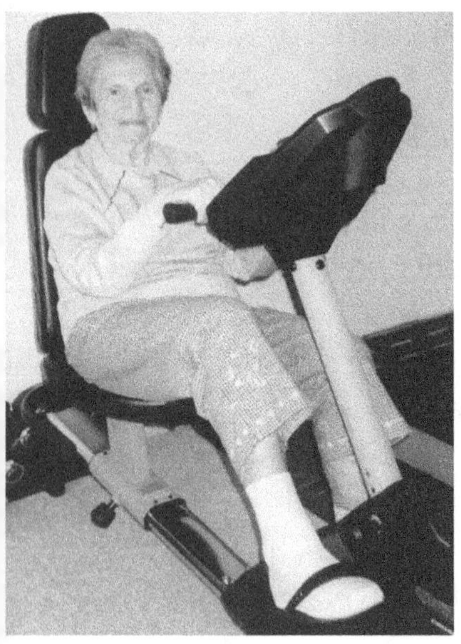

the abyss between their past and present.

California sun beats onto the windows. There is a lump in my throat; I try to put the feeling into words and fail. And then babushka says loudly "rain, rain, go away, come again another day." The existential moment passes and the Chinese lady goes to the treadmill as babushka moves to an arm exercise machine. "Am I molodets?" she asks and I say, "Yes you are, good for you, mom!"

I am glad I got to see

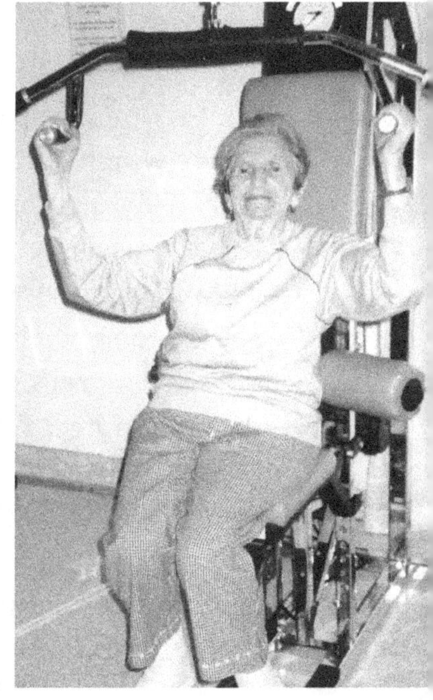

her doing her fitness routine.
For some reason I never saw
her in court when she worked
as a lawyer and now I have no
memory of that.

After her workout, we go upstairs
to her room, I help her change
and we watch a little bit of
Russian TV. I get my usual treat –
"good" Russian chocolate. Now I
feel tired and want to go but she
asks me to stay a bit more and I
do. We don't talk, just watch the
tube. When I get up, she thanks
me, something she started doing
some years ago – a new American
habit. People in the family were
not supposed to thank each other.
I thank her in return and promise

to call tomorrow. When I click her door closed, the lump is in its usual place but then I am outside and sun, trees and street noise take over. Talk to you tomorrow, mom.

AFTERWORD

This story was written in the summer of 2003, the last year of our mom's independent living. In 2004, she had to move to a nursing home because of her failing health. She lived there until her death in January of 2010. "Late for the Train" has a different owner and a different name. "Know Knew Books" closed its doors in 2011, a victim of the digital revolution.

-7-

Hamsa

It was many years ago. We lived in a big communal apartment in the center of Moscow and I was pregnant. According to the medical authorities, everything surrounding labor and birth required the highest levels of hygiene and germ protection, never mind the real state of affairs in crowded hospitals. But rules were rules, so the only people allowed inside delivery and maternity wards were doctors and nurses. I knew I would be one-on-one with Soviet medicine and I needed a plan to get me through.

My simple plan included three points.

Point number one: keep reminding myself that the pain will end just like everything else. This was my modest homegrown philosophical contribution.

Point number two: remember that the French queens had it much worse since, by custom, they were forced to have babies in public, with the royal family and plebes of Paris present. They were under the rule of "noblesse oblige." I, on the other hand, could allow myself misbehavior of all kinds – screaming, begging and being physically violent, if it came to that.

Point number three: I would have an amulet. This thought came from the book by my then favorite author, Lion Feuchtwanger, "The Jew Zuss." The main character was telling the pregnant Duchess the story of Lilith, Eve's predecessor. It turns out Adam couldn't quite make her happy when it came to matters of the flesh. Lilith cursed all love and marriage and ever since, her evil spirit tried to hurt expectant mothers and women in labor. Zuss gave the Duchess a special amulet for protection and she had a healthy baby. Feuchtwanger chose not to provide a description of this amulet.

Why a nonreligious ethnic Jew could be helped by an amulet is a separate subject. But at the end of 1975, I was trying hard to find such a talisman. Not an easy task in the Moscow of that period. My most knowledgeable source was a friend getting ready to emigrate to Israel – a route of escape from the Soviet Union that was recently allowed. After some research, he told me there were no Jewish amulets, but he could get me an Israeli lapel pin. I took him up on his offer.

And so it was – I entered the sterile, equipment-filled labor and delivery room alone, in a regulation hospital gown, bringing the approved piece of chocolate (to have after the birth) and smuggling in my Israeli pin. My daughter was born in February of 1976 after 10 hours of labor, screaming loudly and angrily. From that moment on, my life acquired focus and an unquestionable center of gravity.

It was years later, after our own emigration to the U.S., when I saw Hamsa, a Jewish amulet in the form of a protective hand. My brother-in-law brought me one as a souvenir from Israel. My girlfriend gave me one to hang on the wall. Another friend brought a pretty golden Hamsa to hang over our door.

Many more years later, when my daughter became pregnant and the due date drew near, I remembered my search for an amulet. Suddenly, I knew what to do – Sasha was to have an amulet to protect her during birth. A nice lady in the Jewish store sold me two small Hamsa symbols. Another nice lady in a jewelry shop transformed them into a pair of earrings which were safely packed in Sasha's hospital bag. I prepared my own Hamsa pendant, a gift from Israel, for extra coverage.

When the time came, Sasha and John entered the hospital together. They had their music to comfort

Secret weapon

them, a camera to capture things to come and a computer to connect to the world. The room was full of gentle autumn sunlight, and music played quietly as Sasha and John neared the end of the journey they started nine months before. My granddaughter Athena was born in the evening of a nice warm October day. I heard her loud and angry cry and looked at my exhausted daughter. Two small silver earrings were in her ears, our secret weapon.

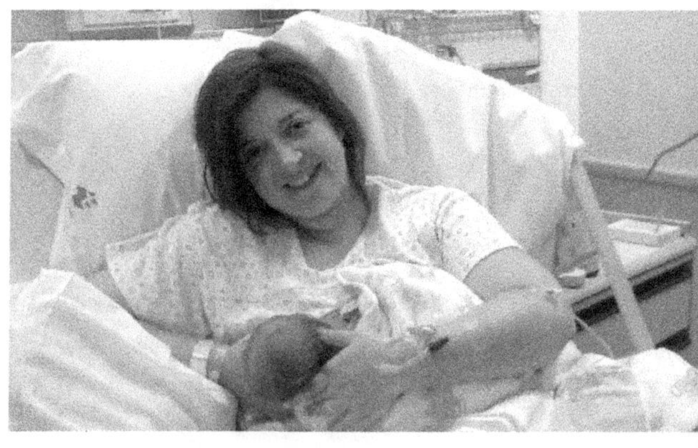

Sasha with Athena in 2008

Acknowledgements

If you find this book easy to read, it's to a large degree due to the competent, steadfast and at the same time gentle editing by Kathy Wilson.

Laura Testa-Reyes, thank you for your unlimited patience dealing with multiple changes.

This book owes its existence to my husband Tom Pencek, my first reader, critic and enthusiastic champion. The book was his idea and he held my hand and directed me through all phases of the publishing process. Thank you, Tommie, for this wonderful gift.

97